A
Man
Against
Time

WILLIAM ELLERY LEONARD

A

Man

Against

Time

AN HEROIC DREAM

New York & London

D. APPLETON-CENTURY COMPANY

INCORPORATED

A
Man
Against
Time

FOREWORD

Plain words be mine, afoot, ahorse, afloat,
That say big things; like that high wooden sign
On Yukon's north bank, near the Porcupine,
Where one reads "ARCTIC CIRCLE" from the boat;
Or Schwitzer's alpine letters pointing south,
"ITALIA," chiselled on the boundary-stone;
Or at the fork, for Trailers facing drouth,
Plains, thunder, Rockies: "ROAD TO OREGON."
Be my words smokeless where they flash or hit,
Aimed not at stalked deer nor at carrion-bird,
But at the Lords — to force, even where they sit,
Surrender from the bleeding gods . . . each word
Edged and compact as steel, steady — and bright
As glint of sunshine on a rifle-sight.

I

O Aphrodite, of all deities
The sole survivor in this iron age
Where temples crumble, sacred fountains freeze,
And men abandon dance and pilgrimage,
O Aphrodite, throned in flowers still,
Though men have mowed their bright heads from
      the lea
To make a place for market, bank, or mill,
Let me proclaim thy naked power on me:
Thou touchest my grey hair to brown again,
Quickenest my eyes to each forgotten star,
Cleansest my shaking white limbs from the fen,
And givest me strength and cunning from afar,
Singing to guide this swift girl leap by leap —
To sing for me great verse upon the steep.

II

We swam from pier to pier across the storm . . .
Then on the sands we watched the golden glow
On cloud and lake, when over us stood a form,
Sudden and lithe and bronze, and said, "Hello."
I matched his shining limbs with yours so white,
His young blue eyes, so buoyant, with your blue,
His dripping hair, all amber in the light,
With yours, belovèd, and you never knew.
O some such life, draining the fresh green earth,
Such strong, free arms, in gorgeous interplay,
Should follow yours in one triumphant mirth,
And dance your beauty down a long, long way . . .
And yet for you and me the sun was warm,
And yet we swam together in the storm.

III

My love for you has been distilled by time
Of many simples: of sunset, hill, and lake,
Of dead blue eyes, a dead voice, and an ache
Of thirty years, of fragments of great rhyme
Saved from the poets in my singing prime,
Of sea-stars rising on the liner's wake,
And of the boy in me that still would make
His dreams of what is lovely and sublime
Peal forth as from a tower . . . This love for you
Is all the best of all I've lived or won —
How very old it seems, and still how new,
As if the unguessed end of all I'd done.
And yet your love's so selfless, golden, fine,
Earth and her flowers will count it more than mine.

IV

This love of ours treads down no other love,
Today's or yesterday's; and, dear, no other
Can tread on this: for this, if not above,
Is yet apart from friend, wife, child, or mother:
Its sudden, fiery coming, like the sun
Over the arctic snows, is my own youth,
With light renewed and speech again begun,
Restive and strong for beauty, goodness, truth;
And its keen eyes that pierce my silent pain,
And know my greying age as none has known,
Give your young voice the themes I try in vain,
And you are me today, your speech my own.
It's all so strange and holy . . . and apart . . .
A brave new sanctity of life and art.

V

I'd love your spirit, trailing on, apart
From your white body: like a new voice sprung
In Paradise from Beatricë's heart,
With mercy and wisdom in old Italian tongue.
I'd love your body apart: thrusting with knees
To open a pathway between reed and reed,
Like some lost marble of Praxiteles
Smit by the Sungod into warmth and speed.
In either suddenly I'd find my fate —
In beauty of either find magnificence
Enough, delight enough, to make me great,
With either's plenitude for soul and sense.
Now, loving both, each giving each increase,
I own in you cathedral aisles and Greece.

VI

Lovely white hands, what memories you bring
Of ladies' hands I saw where I was bred:
Of Sappho's hands, darting from string to string;
And Lesbia's hands, cupping her sparrow dead;
And Héloïse's, turning in lonely hours
Those songs once sung through all the realm of
     France;
Persephone's hands, braiding Sicilian flowers;
Diana's hands, twin leaders in the dance;
Nausicaa's hands, clutching her golden clasp;
Penelope's, weaving with a shuttle-toss;
And Cleopatra's hands on breast and asp;
And hands of Mary Mother at the cross . . .
Dearest, your hands, so lovely, loving, white —
May they hold my hands on my last goodnight . . .

VII

Great Abélard and greater Héloïse,
Thrice sacred dust to me: in student-days
I sought your tomb alone in Père-Lachaise
(Forsaking other names and effigies);
Then in midmanhood of my long disease
I read your letters — questions, prayers, and praise —
Words of two friends with high and tragic ways,
Who talked from Latin folios on my knees.
But, lovers dead eight hundred years ago,
I've loved you fully first since loving her —
This girl to whom my grey-haired verses go:
You're now both nearest of all things that were,
Though in my halls new winds of doctrine blow,
Sans Matins, Mary, Cross, or Comforter.

VIII

Time is the great king whom is no gainsaying:
I'm sturdier than my years, yet I am old,
And you, how young with all your red and gold,
And lithe as Pan upon a white birch swaying!
Measure your dimples by the wrinkles playing
About my eyes; your Hopes, so naked, bold,
By my long Quiet, mantled fold on fold;
Your laughter by my irony; your Maying
By my October:
                    Time is king. And yet . . .
I know and you know there is one strange shore
(How few have ever in its woodlands met)
Where time can seal his grey decrees no more;
And two freed vassals there, defiers of
Time and his power: my love, dear child, your love.

You're twenty-four tonight . . . in mid-December.
Did Nature, appointing you this bleak birthday,
With never a bird or flower, not remember
You had a destined rendezvous with May?
Or did she plan me recompense for grey
Horizons and the grate with ashen ember? —
O you blithe singer on the leafless spray,
Who make my springtime even in mid-December.
Or was it she guessed that any month would suit,
With its own excellence, to give you birth? —
Who share with her each season of the earth . . .
Season of blossoms, or of ripening fruit,
Or harvest sunsets, or when high in heaven
Sparkle the winter Pleiades, all seven.

X

Is there not something greater than I knew
In the long travail of star, sun, and earth?
In death of empires to give empires birth,
While off beyond their walls the wildflowers grew?
Something still lovelier in the rainbow, too,
Arched on the silver sky or waterfall? —
Else how could I, who thought I knew them all,
So in my grey years shake on knowing you?
What are you, then? An island in the sea?
Laughter outwitting and outwinging tears?
Tears that aflood roll laughter down the rocks?
You're pillow, fire, rest, anguish unto me:
All this is simple . . . but my wiseman's ears
Ring with new sound that awes, exalts me, mocks.

The only gods at last are those of Greece!
I know, I know, — whether in wood or cave,
Or on the hills, or rising from the wave . . .
O their great eyelids both in war and peace!
The only gods at last are those of Greece!
For they alone are competent to save
Both soul and body, out above the grave,
And give to flesh and spirit one release
Of joy and health. O come again, O walk
Here with this girl and me! Ye will not chide,
If sometimes most I love her tender talk,
And sometimes most the white skin on her side;
And we both need you in these alien lands
Of sterile gods and prayers with bony hands.

XII

O ye strong fellows of the early earth,
Who on the waves and winds of Homer's Greek
Still lift your lances and still hoist your sails,
Still fight my battles and still voyage with me,
O ye great creatures, peerless in your worth
Whether to feast, to pray, to fight, to seek,
Who make more blue the fresh Aegean gales,
And make the sun, by shining on you, be
A sun more golden, O ye strong and bold,
Give me, give me, a beaten man and old,
In these far, inland years, give me at length
Across the continents and centuries, friends,
O something of your youth, your hope, your strength,
To give in turn this girl . . . before life ends.

XIII

I've lived through night to see the morning star
Here from this craghead, where long hours the wave
Hurled geysers up the clefts, and scooped the grave
For the masted hull that brought me here from far.
I've lived through night to see the morning star
Shine where the clouds are hollowed to a cave,
Like one fixed altar-candle down a nave ...
But keen as bright tip of a scimitar.
I've lived through night to see the morning star.
The clouds roll off to darken another sea.
Wait, star, but one blue minute still for me,
Ere day ride forth on Homer's golden car,
And your intense, unflinching point of white
Sets in the blaze of circumambient light.

XIV

O be my voice, belovèd, or I die!
There's thirty years of silence clogs my throat —
Such truth unspoken, deep, new, glorious, high,
Which strangles me, each throb an unsung note —
Truth born of living ... few have lived as I ...
Crowned by the logic of our white embrace,
And by blue crystal fires within your eye,
When you look murmuring to my tortured face.
Belovèd, righteous lips, be soon my lips!
Ev'n more than your kiss shall be your speech for me:
I'm chained, I'm barred, I'm cowed by iron whips,
But you are young, are strong, are brave, are free ...
And none who speak have known (or loved) me so—
O be my voice that all mankind may know.

II

XV

I hear two voices in life's afternoon,
Belovèd, like two singing stars unseen.
One from lost morning: "Man, your east had been
A glorious passage, had you met her soon."
One from the coming dusk behind the blue,
Belovèd: "Man, already in your west,
What of her journey when you go to rest —
The woman who finds her east and west in you?"
Two troubling voices, crossing the oblique light
Of the great sun still excellently bright . . .
But a third voice, as from a shining tree
With roots in earth deep as its branching height,
Starts its glad music so much nearer me,
That I forget those other voices quite.

XVI

You're all best daughters of the great white race
That ship by ship set sail and bred new towns,
And with its cart-wheels grooved old plains and
    downs,
And with sown wheat drove trees before its face;
You're all best daughters in each dwelling-place,
Greek island, Danube, or the prairies west —
As of its elder sons I'm all the best,
And feel in right arm axe, scythe, spear, lyre, mace ...
We should beget together. We should be
Forebears of generations tall and blond,
Muscled for heaving, chinned and eyed for speech;
But, aching in our balked fecundity,
We sit here sterile by this inland pond ...
While one more sunset darkens over each.

XVII

Suppose, when need of woman first shook me
Walking the upland orchards, I'd met you
Coming for apples, what a man I'd be
Today with your breasts having helped me through!
The life, in your translucent body cased,
Down my dark past unwitting sends a light,
Whereby I see how bleak and blown that waste,
How needless, had earth timed our years aright.
Yet why not shout in late delight and pride
That, blasting my way through fate and natural laws,
My grey has won such gold before I died? —
Why not? — O desperate, loving mate, because
I've launched your girlhood on a winter tide . . .
And on my oars ice thickens in the flaws.

XVIII

My kin all dead, my childless house a hall
Of spells and spectres deforming the windowed sun,
Friends few or far, and passing one by one,
My body yoked here like an ox in stall
By long disease, and my free spirit thrall
By poverty to codes and creeds outrun,
My unregarded life-work done . . . done . . . done . . .
This is my state at last . . . nor is this all . . .
And now you've come to me, belovèd friend:
You're mother, sister, daughter, quite beside
The love that's like a lover's for a bride,
And, dear, as each I'd love you without end.
What of your life, then, being all the four? . . .
It's dangerous coming to a need so sore.

XIX

In whom can I burrow? Who'll enfold my ache?
My naked weakness needs again the womb:
In whom can I huddle, stirring? O in whom
But only you? — although your body shake . . .
Then to be born again, then to awake,
Plenished with your blood in that fertile gloom,
To try life over, with more light and room
And your arms hugging all I undertake . . .
O Mother-spirit of love, ultimate rest
Not only, but communicative power,
It's your great need to womb me for that birth,
That, thus re-manned, through spiritual incest
I grow your mate and master of our Hour,
Dear Mother-spirit of love, my Mother-earth.

XX

The solemn difference in our years, fates, beings,
Makes love do different work on you and me,
Even though from one hill all our suns and seeings
And one our spray of blossoms from each tree.
On me, so parched by death and ugly thirst,
Long in an iron trap with hundred teeth,
Love's work is peace and beauty (Dear, my first),
Except my fears for you that coil beneath.
For love has crashed, like lightning on a rose,
And shakes afire your sinews, marrow, blood,
And starts the mother-milk in breasts, with throes
Like childbirth on the waters of a flood.
Dear, help me calm your tumult . . . for my sake . . .
Lest love's last work on both should be: to break.

XXI

Why is it, in absence when your love I feel
And your soft flesh of tenderness and joy,
I founder with intrusive thoughts of steel,
Iron and carbon's fiery fixed alloy?
Why is it, when striving to rhyme out anew
The marrow, the structure of your living bone,
I've these obsessing visions in the blue
Of interlacing girders set in stone?
Why is it, recalling how we clung together,
Up my horizon rides the dreadnaught's keel,
With plates, guns, conning-tower in shining weather,
One menace of intolerable steel? —
Steel's twice our symbol, as we love, fear, doubt:
Of strength we need within — and see without.

This evening-lake turns stale for eyes, nose, hands.
Come, Thor or Thrymr, out of Morningheim,
And bowl that low round sun, from where he stands,
Down the long ridge! Burn all to steam and lime!
Then, in this emptied valley, charred and new,
Pour me the sea from atoll, bay, or fjord,
Far from green sewage! Pour the brine, the blue,
With palms, or whales, or icebergs swirling toward!
Since first I met this woman in these woods,
This sky and earth contract in all four quarters;
My love's outgrown these inland quietudes,
And needs the smell of salt on winds and waters.
Or, Thor and Thrymr, pile these narrow shores
With mountains, granite sides and lava cores.

XXIII

Above this marsh and stench of green decay,
With here and there a lily shining white,
Rises this hill of ours whereon we stay,
Stay evermore, in high primordial light
Made by the sun, made by the moon. This hill
Is granite outcrop and this light thereon
Is younger only than the stars, and will
Survive this marsh till sun and moon are gone.
Taking my hand, you say: "With light from space
I feel our love has kinship, beauty, awe,
And with the granite outcrop of this place —
As something bright and stark as cosmic law.
Believe that love can last as long as light
And granite can communicate its might!"

XXIV

Exist these poems for me or I for them?
Am I here giving life and love new speech,
As my lost spirit's desperate stratagem
Where life and love themselves exceed my reach?
Or am I old Earth's aching instrument,
A throat, compounded of her roots and clays,
To clarify her unfulfilled intent
On man and woman in these latter days?
Exist these poems for you or you for these?
Exist they to sustain you in your tears?
Or are you beauty-in-pain on bended knees
As a fresh theme to quicken my sterile years?
Whatever the answer, I'd give them to the dead —
Might I but build a house around our bed.

XXV

Let's build a hilltop shack with green-felled pines
From my New Hampshire woodlot . . . and then
    sleep.
I want to wake beside your nakedness
Just one high morning in the clear bright air,
And see to east, as your Chaldean friend,
With you the sunrise in the Zodiac,
And see to west its light on steeple-dial
Far down the valley, as vacationer
With you, my friend, from reaping, spinning,
    milking,
Of yesterday's America . . . Then with you,
My friend, to breed a manchild who will plant
In his own season honest corn, and mould
From your lips and from mine his honest speech
Of old traditions and new prophecies.

We're each such proud eyes, Dawn and Eve on fire,
Each tongue a bodkin, either's will like oak,
Each with a moody and insurgent lyre:
Say, *could* Love use us two as married folk?
If Love so could, and build harmonious days
In one small tent with milk, bread, mutton, cheese,
And close our tent-flap on each prying face,
Would Love not then achieve his masterpiece?
On this tribe's grazing-grounds we'll never know
(And where's another Whither — and how — to
    flee?),
Nor know what goodly sire and dam we'd be,
But only feel together: 'twould be so . . .
Giving each other all we have to give,
It's yet by acts of faith we mostly live.

XXVII

Enough for us is each day's loneliness,
Meeting by moments only, and those broken,
Without fore-living the supreme distress
When once our bodily goodbyes are spoken.
O might what we of future pangs now borrow
Take something of their substance when they come,
Subduing our todays that that tomorrow
May not too fiercely with its ache benumb.
But this is fool's arithmetic. The ache,
Foreknown, foredreaded, will be there fourfold,
When each is wandering in a separate city:
An ache in each of selfhood and heartbreak,
An ache for the other's ache untold or told,
In helpless longing and in helpless pity.

XXVIII

Names of vast cities off beyond your tears—
Ahmednagar, Bangkok, and Bangalore,
Kerbela, Chinkiang, Kharkov, and Algiers,
And Banyuwangi, Kostroma, Lahore;
Names of vast cities off beyond my fears—
Shimonoseki, Santos, Singapore,
Tananarivo, Saskatoon, Namirs,
And Pernambuco, Nice, San Salvador;
Names of vast cities off beyond our love—
Mosul, Mendoza, Tucuman, Dijon,
Guadalajara, Pavia, and Rostov,
Rosario, Santander, Edmonton . . .
With Buddha-bells, spires, minarets — more far
Than our last moon or sessions with a star.

There works a tremulous tightening on your lip,
And quivers a swelling blue film in your eyes,
Because not even your loving mastership
(So selfless, crimson, confident, and wise)
Has won the glory of its supreme hope
To free my years and give me back the feet
To roam the Rhine and see upon the slope
Of Alps again the sunrise, or to beat
Down the long ocean winds (with you) to Spain;
A tightening and a tear, because (this too)
Your visions, love, and music throb in vain
(Or yet not quite?) to rouse my art anew:
Too long inured to mockeries of relief,
I only grieve today for your young grief.

XXX

Our sonnets are written with our commingled blood,
A crimson script where still our arteries throb;
And sometime searchers for the great and good
Will find and know them, startled to a sob
Of exultation; yes, such folk will show
These sonnets for a patient brave device
That captured glory against the uplifted 'No'
Of Circumstance — O more than once or twice!
They'll say: "This man's and woman's rhymes in red
Were their sea-voyaging to the Parthenon,
Their trail along the Rockies' watershed,
Their dance with Islanders to greet the sun" . . .
They'll say: "These sonnets are the child they bred,
When Knives had splayed and cut them and undone."

XXXI

If there's no help in verse for you and me,
If there's no salvage in our art from pain,
Where then is help? And where shall be the gain? —
The Muse alone, for those condemned as we
To narrow anguish and sterility,
Can be the goddess of a faith not vain.
She shall be merciful to you again,
As long ago to Sappho by the sea.
Beyond these streets, beyond each insolent spire,
O far beyond, there lies a white plateau:
Think yourself there! — lifting a golden lyre
High in your arm to take the afterglow
From distant glaciers all one pagan fire . . .
And hear her footsteps cross the brittle snow.

XXXII

Tonight I'm bleak as heaving ice that takes
The wash of polar seas, or lava plains
Cracked on the cold dead moon whose fiery lakes
Were crusted to stone before the oldest grains
Or ferns of earth; I hear the planets spin,
But cannot see their sun; and from afar,
Beyond Andromeda and every star
I feel the tides of darkness closing in.
But do not chide, belovèd, do not sorrow:
Sometimes a pang from your young love and laughter
Sinks my grey years in the before and after,
But this will pass when in your arms tomorrow.
Be ready for my head upon your breast . . .
And lay away this stanza with the rest.

XXXIII

The bell tolls midnight from the Campus-tower,
And one more day is done for you and me.
This afternoon alone I sat an hour
Where bright October rippled this inland sea,
And golden sun on oak and hickory
Became the echo of your voice, with power
Almost to make me young again and free
To walk the far woods for the one last flower
Before the winter ... Midnight ... And I keep
My lonely room, and read the Odyssey:
It's where Odysseus (in book twenty-three),
Home after twice ten years on land and deep,
Tells all his story to Penelope,
In their old bridal bed before they sleep.

XXXIV

This day is in no calendar; its hours
Are fragments risen from the days gone under:
This rain on leafless elms, with winter thunder;
This lake unfrozen, margined by no flowers;
And in my eyes, on looking out of doors,
This tearless pain of boyhood memories,
When first I read how Byron died in Greece,
And Shelley's corpse gleamed on the sandy shores
Of Italy . . . And where, on this weird day,
Are you, belovèd? — Gone where I can't follow —
With brooding forethought all your own, to lay
Two roses on an old grave in a hollow,
Dug for a woman, in your infancy,
Whom you now love because she so loved me.

XXXV

No, no, unsay me that! — You shall not die,
No, not with my death, which, however late,
Must come while still there's daybreak in your eye.
No, no, unsay me that, but say you'll wait!
Wait, golden twenty-four, till gold is white!
'Twill be an echoing interval of time:
For you're of those the green earth fashioned right,
To take her fruits and give her back a rhyme.
And, golden twenty-four, remember, too,
That, though so tired, I'll hate to leave the sun;
But that, with now so much of me in you,
Death can't be death for me while you live on.
When my hour comes, be competent and brave,
And give me fifty years beyond my grave.

III

XXXVI

When sea-born Aphrodite rode the foam,
Poised in the west-wind on the fluted shell
That bore her toward Cyprus, her first home,
Not even the elder gods observed her well:
They saw her wring her wild hair, wipe the brine
From lips and lids, yes, saw her smile and haste
To unloose the seaweeds from her breasts and twine
Thereof a girdle for her navelled waist —
With a mock modesty . . . But their weak eyes
Saw not her fingers press the ooze and spray
From golden-tufted cleft between her thighs
(Though even earth's flowers quickened far away),
That throbbing cleft which took Anchises' seed —
Whence burst Aeneas and the Roman breed.

XXXVII

It's age, not youth, alone can truly love:
Only when thought has mastered sex and found
It one with treetops, hills, and stars above,
One with all roots, springs, minerals underground,
Only when grief again, again, has laid
Hot hands upon cold bodies of our dead,
Can man approach love truly unafraid,
And know the warmth and whispers of love's bed;
And only a man who's clambered many a peak,
And heard the lava boil, the vapor hiss,
Or walked burnt cities in the flame and reek,
Can pour a life-time in a single kiss.
Against all poets I would stake this truth,
Except your love for me is born — of youth.

XXXVIII

A man who, late in years, first eyes the sea,
Or moonrise over palms in island blue,
Will startle that for him there still can be,
In spite of all he's pondered or been through,
Something so unimaginably new
For sight, for insight, and for ecstasy:
And so, belovèd, is it now with me
Before the fresh white nakedness of you.
Loving your body, suddenly I know
How a young mother, bathing her first-born,
Delights in human flesh anew each morn:
Its shape, its motions, its soft skin aglow,
So seized by living beauty, pulse, smile, breath,
She cannot think of Time and Change and Death.

XXXIX

I never knew a heart that beat so fast,
Seeing a wild rose or the harvest moon,
Or paint and marble statues of the past,
Or naked children by the salt-sea dune;
I never knew a back that trembled so,
Reading some poet by the lamp-lit shelf —
Except in one lone cottage long ago,
When I was living with my younger self.
My pulse has cost me dear; but I'm the male,
My thews the tougher from stern bouts with scorn:
O gentle, loving heart-beat, woman-born,
May your white body be not all too frail . . .
Feel, feel my good arms round you when you ache,
Beat, beat on my heart, sleeping or awake.

XL

When on the rug you sit between my knees,
With upturned lids and speechless parted lips,
And I lean down toward silent melodies,
Nesting in your gold hair my fingertips,
Which of us two, in love's old posture thus,
The bridal lady or her learnèd lord,
The blue eyes or the brown eyes, — which of us
Is here the adoring one, is here the adored?
If mocking spirit of insolent casuistry
Will have a subtle answer, here it is:
You gaze as into sky, I into sea,
Yet each of us explores the same abyss,
Where I get lost in you and you in me,
And every this is that and that is this.

These verses stand in praise of chastity,
Though I'm no monk, no Milton, nor no Paul.
Yield, amorous nun, who on thy aching knee
Prayest the blue-robed Virgin in the wall;
Yield, virtuous maid, who at thy trysting tree
Knowest to kiss and fondle — and not fall;
Yield, too, ye pure in proud frigidity,
Yield to my lady, chaster than ye all! —
Who takes a fire, first lit in bird and beast,
And, passing it through her body, sets it free
To flame in temples; makes her love the priest
To sanctify that body unto me —
As clean as swaying petals, or foam at sea,
When, after rain, the sun is in the east.

XLII

Yes, zone by zone your body now I know:
Tousled gold hair on head erect and free;
Blue fire of eyes that say, "I see, I see";
The arch lips pursing to a sudden "Oh";
Your white breasts nippled by two buds; the fresh
Soft hollows where their shadowed crescents be;
The elastic torso of your navelled flesh,
Blent with your fine hips' brave anatomy;
The golden tuft between the veinèd thighs;
The calves of Artemis in step or pose,
Echoing the motions of your arms and eyes —
O form, all grace from fingertips to toes,
Some light, strength, speed, from river, wind, and
        star
Became your soul and made you what you are.

XLIII

I talk to your sleeping body, kneeling by:
"White body, I stake you for sheer ecstasy
Upon me, acquainted with beauty though I be,
Against each lovely thing of earth or sky,
Sea-wave, cloud, fire, or heron streaming high,
Against all gold of flower, or sun, or tree —
Lithe body, you bright morning unto me,
Just when I felt my evening drawing nigh.
But, body, my teacher of what Nature is,
Round you I draw a super-natural line,
Not as most lovely, body, but for this:
As the one thing in the whole world wholly mine,
Dear body, good to look on, good to keep" . . .
I talk to your body (did you hear, asleep?).

If, dear, so late I learn from side to side
Your body (though my palms and pupils follow
So often its every curve and bone and hollow
That now I seem its sculptor in my pride),
How soon, then, can I learn your mind, my bride? —
Quick though I be to know the deep from shallow
And whether a soul is germinant or fallow,
And though you've not a root or spring you'd hide . . .
Yes, I assemble data: joke and tear,
Those whom you love, those whom you hate — and
     why,
Your books, your pictures, your own sturdy scrawl;
But when down, down your honest eyes I peer,
To world on world each with its sun and sky,
I think I'll never, never learn it all.

XLV

Naked you make my naked lap your bed,
White twenty-four in tawny fifty-seven,
Drooping your noble, your defiant head,
Baffled by Why and Whither of what's given;
My answers seem to you like withered flowers
Uprooted in the noonday, dead at dusk,
A bowl of milk that in the thunder sours,
Or nubbins, blue and blighted in the husk.
You cling so close, as if you begged me give
Wisdom directly from my blood and bone—
Something authentic, warm, and primitive,
As old as searching fire or lasting stone . . .
Dear, make your subtle body hear and see—
And, if my body tells you aught, tell me.

You give me much to ponder, and I you
(Breathing each other's body, curve, throb, vein,
Diving down eyes into each other's brain);
And Earth, despite her blunders, made us two
Deft to weave thoughts from all we find or do.
Sometimes we weave together from one skein,
Sometimes in lonely Afterwards from twain —
As this which starlight helped me weave anew:
"Two loves in womankind are manifest, —
One, to-possess — and one, to-be-possessed.
This eats the man till love and he are gone,
That gives to eat till love and he are one.
And love-to-be-possessed alone can give
Love-to-possess a pure prerogative."

XLVII

Your love for me is music, with a range
Of many octaves in one melody,
With tempos that forever subtly change,
Yet all organic as a symphony,
Now loud, now low, inveterate in brain,
And holding ever to its major key,
Yet with two moments dominant and main —
Crescendos of exalted ecstasy:
The one where, quickened by your power, I read
To you my first rhymes, after silent years;
The other where first I came into your bed
And in your white arms first forgot my fears —
Two moments where that music on the heights
Shoots up the heavens like the northern lights.

XLVIII

When first I had you in your nakedness,
My grey years shook, bewildered, dazzled, prone:
Your body's beauty, joy, and eagerness
Came from a living morning long unknown.
I had not mastered so divine a place,
So suddenly such eyes and loins and knees,
Had I not read in your transfigured face
I was the god of your idolatries.
O what a cult we founded on that night:
A god and goddess worshipping each other,
And mutually establishing a rite
Whereby each made diviner still the other.
How long ago all this . . . Now we enfold
Because our limbs are warm — and the world cold.

Strangest of all things in my long strange time,
To lie with your young limbs abed and talk—
Backs propped on pillow, hand upon your breast,
Before or after, quiet in embrace—
Of Shakespeare's heroines or Shelley's rhyme,
Of how the shellfish formed the Dover-chalk,
Of why Columbus set his sails to west,
And what today the Russians plan apace
Defying Cross and Coin, of the Sublime
Discussed by him Longinus, of the walk
Of lecturing Aristotle, Plato's quest,
Odysseus' shoulders, Sappho's lyric face.
Strangest of all things how your sex and youth
Wake a man's nakedness to speak its truth.

L

So mid-December now means twenty-five,
Your silver wedding, dear, with Life and me:
For that first Morning when you came alive
Involved you in that holy bigamy.
I mean I loved you from the cradle-edge,
Through dreaming girlhood, down to this our bed,
And stood and gave to Morning there my pledge,
Along with Life, and kept what then I said.
But you reply, with quick Shakespearian twist
That makes old words and thoughts adroitly new:
"But, lover mine, I'm not a bigamist
Today — for Life itself's now only you" . . .
For your sake, then, enfold me, nourish, cover . . .
Yet when I die may Life be still your lover.

LI

I do believe these poems encompass more
In brave, fair honesty of love-report
Than ever artist dared, tried, did before,
Whether in country-side, or bower, or court;
For Life that's been so hard on me gives this:
At fifty-seven still youth enough to feel,
With practiced vigor of analysis,
And speech to match bold insight in the real.
Touching this last: a man at fifty-seven,
Like me who's watched so long each coward neighbor
Live with blurred eyeballs in a tinsel heaven,
Finds seeing-clear a joy and not a labor.
Moreover, few poets have had a chance to see
An Aphrodite in Antigone.

My fathers shored house-timbers on the rocks,
Timbers of oak with oaken timbers shored,
Based on New Hampshire's windward mountain-
    blocks
With torrents, frosts, and lightnings scarred and
    scored.
Large-handed Puritans whom these flabby years
Disdain with easy jibes, they being dead;
Stiff-necked come-outers, ruthless pioneers,
What did they do, on corn and ginger fed? —
Settling one kingdom east, they built the west
With ox-carts; built the school-house, voting-booth,
Fought that democracy be more than jest,
And gnawed the slave's chains with a madman's tooth.
Come-outers, pioneers! — and I'm their son,
Though Greek-schooled like Monadnock-Emerson.

LIII

I long to bore in earth and plunge in fire,
For the one's darkness and the other's light,
For tree-roots, for stone-base of mountain-height,
For each telluric Under propping Higher;
For core of flame inside its cone or spire,
Where motion splits from motion out of sight,
Which makes the sun and radiations right
Whence plants get peace and animals desire.
I long to plunge in fire and bore in earth —
But most for dead-folk. Dear, these elements
Hold Druid whispers, roaring caravan,
Battles and weddings, infants, music, mirth,
And all abandoned feasts and parliaments
Since graves and pyres have been the house of man.

Train, ye proud wise men, your great telescope
Upon Andromeda, in earth's cool nights
Where California's rainless mountain-heights
Rise over bartering cities and their hope.
Train that imperious eye upon all space,
And tell me what it tells you, in your dome,
Of galaxies, light-years, and worlds-to-come,
And where amid stars is the sun's dwelling-place,
And earth's . . . Then turn from Upward-outward,
        men,
To Downward. Plumb the neighbor-rocks and probe
What's under foot: what news beneath the hill?
Ye bore a rim of iron and oxygen,
Granite and fire . . . that's all. Earth's little globe
Withholds us knowledge of her centre still.

Ocean: whale-shoulder and octópus-arm,
Brown Polynesians on volcanic rock;
Then, with no buoy to whistle the alarm,
The engulfing tidal-wave, the earthquake shock.
Ocean: the trireme with the long black oars,
The Viking sail with red stripes bellying round,
The gay Titanic headed for our shores,
The valiant Lusitania eastward bound.
Ocean: above her ever half the sky,
Ever the Dipper or the Southern Cross.
Ocean: beneath her in the darkness lie
What lengths of sand far-littered with our loss.
But, Love, take heart: ten million years will show
All dry and cleared — like the Sahara now.

LVI

How hast thou grown, Death, since begot and born
Of the first Protozoans in the slime!
Thou rangest, the most tremendous birth of Time,
Mocking the prophet's call, the hunter's horn,
The radio's proclamations night and morn,
Or Latin hymns, hexameter and rhyme,
Taller than mountains, bigger-necked than Crime,
Master of Life itself, though Life's first-born.
Thou gott'st new bulk, as fed with worm, fish, lizard,
Amphibian, bird, mammal; and in rocks
Thy fossil-footprints spread . . . huger each one . . .
But only when came Man, in flood and blizzard
Crossing the vales, or battling for gold or flocks,
Wert thou almighty as thy foe, the Sun.

LVII

Though crippled, prisoned, white-haired, fifty-eight,
My world a heap of ashes, splinters, shards,
Until I die, by God, I'll stand up straight—
And when I die I want no flowers and cards.
What have I seen? I've seen the Caesars come,
The work of Athens and Rome's Senate free
And parliaments of centuries stricken dumb,
And upstarts spitting on democracy.
I've seen man's speech, which Time had won for art
Since Homer clear and clean and serving man,
Distorted, maimed, and in the insane mart
The laurel-crown on every charlatan.
I'll stand up straight, not to rebuke these years—
But for my faith in my abandoned peers.

LVIII

I'd shake your hand, mad Alcibiades . . .
Not for your youth, wit, beauty sent by Zeus,
Nor for eristic learned from Socrates,
Nor scarcely for your ships at Syracuse;
But since we both disdain the dainty flute,
Because it shuts our eyes, distorts the cheek,
And makes the lips for glorious talking mute.
Let Thebans pipe who know not how to speak —
Give me a harp. Yes, we Athenian Knights
Would keep our vision, faces, and our tongue;
Athena's still the guardian of our heights,
Apollo still protector of our young:
One threw the flute away, with upturned chin;
The other stripped the Flute-player of his skin.

The Cid's my man. Not he of Corneille's play—
All Alexandrines, honor, strut, and roar—
But that stern Doer of an earlier day,
The Juglar's Cid, mio Cid, el Campeador;
Mio Cid, my Cid, of Castile's market-places,
In epic-balladry, whose music beat
Its grief and glory on the crowded faces
And sent those Spaniards home on sturdier feet.
His king exiled him, and on horse he sped
With his few faithful over the frontier,
Fought 'gainst the Moors to gain his daily bread,
And won Valencia with his pennoned spear;
Led wife and daughters with him up its towers—
And said: "These plains are mine, are yours, are
   ours."

LX

Master Lucretius, have we gained on you
In these two thousand years of probe and speech,
Of song and science, with our vaster view,
And each voice through the centuries tutoring each?
We know dimensions of the Milky Way,
How sun, earth, moon are but pale dots therein;
We've Virgil, Dante, Milton, since your day,
And Goethe, too, to help us to begin.
Yet silent before the universe we are,
Gaping like children staring at an urn;
And when we'd hear the echoes of a star,
Even to this hour to you we have to turn.
But, Master Lucretius, as to woman's love,
You come to me — and I'll sing you thereof.

LXI

Where's the dividing line, dear Love, between
Ancient and Modern? How false man's calendar
Which splits old times from new by that lone star
At Bethlehem, of Hebrew shepherds seen.
Horse, coach, and sail still served man's to-and-fro;
Herbs, plasters, magic still were cures; bare hands
Still reaped, spun, wove, and smithied in all lands . . .
Even as in Troy . . . two hundred years ago.
Shall we divide by when gunpowder flamed,
By when Columbus mapped the world anew,
Copernicus the skies, by when first blew
Whistles of steam, or lightnings first were tamed? —
Whatever Earth's date of After-and-Before,
We two know ours and can't revise that lore.

LXII

I turn a walnut knob and hear all earth:
Isolde's Liebestod sobbed from Bayreuth;
The Pope proclaiming marriage, sex, and birth,
In Cicero's Latin periods answering Freud;
The Prince of Wales pleading for London slums;
Hitler defying all Geneva's choice;
Il Duce's fifes and the Mikado's drums;
And Roosevelt's deciding, faithful voice.
Last Christmas the Judaean bell I heard
From tower in Bethlehem, south of Galilee;
Last night the flagship of our Admiral Byrd,
With laboring whistle in Antarctic sea.
But there's no sound so far away, so near,
No miracle like your lips against my ear.

While earthquakes now engulf both old and new —
Dug-up Persepolis and Babylon,
Along with topless towers of steel and stone
At Paris and Manhattan in the blue;
While tidal waves, with lightnings from the main,
Drown forts, thrones, halls of justice, on each shore,
And craters, silent since the dinosaur,
Belch inland fire and ash on fruits and grain;
Now while mankind in every braggart clan,
With envy of their fellow's singèd rags,
Take to the farthest caverns that they can,
With patriot banners and frayed money-bags;
Now while the earth and nations heave and sink,
We two report: "Love loves even on the brink."

LXIV

The gametes joining, by an unsolved spell
That works the same in every million wombs,
Do form one zygote out of sperm and cell
And of their halved, uniting chromosomes.
So in the protozoan lowliest union,
Whence blastula and embryo unfold,
We find that action of the sex-communion,
That one-from-two, which Jesus named of old.
O man-and-woman, who become one flesh,
Dream, in a deep sleep after passion spent,
Of that next fusion whence life starts afresh,
And may your dreams presage a high event:
A son with brain to solve how these things be,
Or poet to meditate the mystery.

LXV

Today begins our third spring, Dearest, Only;
And Time and Love are winning over speech.
Yes, Verse with breaking knees, a lost and lonely
Runner in light, with arms in desperate reach
Forward to Love and Time, gasps with dry breath,
Cannot catch up, nay, more and more's behind.
For Love and Time, O friend, like Life and Death,
Mock Art and shake my confidence in mind . . .
Now Art is falling in the long, bright dust
Defeated; and it sees far, far ahead
Time and great Love, and, fallen, knows it must
Perish with half the wonderful unsaid.
This is our third spring . . . and the sun is back
For one more journey through the Zodiac.

LXVI

Wise men with spades two thousand years from now
Will find our bones and two skulls face to face;
And, measuring pelvic girdle, skinless brow,
Will jot: "Male, female, of Caucasian race . . ."
And then they'll box them, having scraped and dried.
And none will strew one thought on their old fate —
As whether these bones, so locked there side by side,
Drank death in ecstasy of love or hate.
Those wise won't know how once on that same hill
Your white limbs burst through sunset and swept
    down,
Detaching in a lustrous miracle
Streamers of gold and crimson for your gown,
And danced those waters with each twinkling knee,
Swaying, all light and motion, on — to me.

LXVII

With most sound mind I make my testament:
To you, my all of what the sun and sea,
Mountain and thunder, flower and lake and tree
For fifty bold and thwarted years have meant;
To you, each unsung song, each high event
Imagined in my long captivity, —
The incorruptible deep self of me . . .
To you, each unaccomplished merriment.
To you, that strength, when I am dead, to live,
As I still lived when one I loved had died;
That, out of what you are, and what I give
With Love as sage attorney by my side,
You make another Love-song — line by line
Far overarching, like a rainbow, mine.

Grateful acknowledgment is made to *American Mercury, American Prefaces, College Verse, Modern Monthly, The New Republic,* and *The Saturday Review of Literature* for permission to include in this volume certain sonnets which originally appeared in those periodicals.

BY WILLIAM ELLERY LEONARD

POETRY

A MAN AGAINST TIME

THIS MIDLAND CITY

A SON OF EARTH

TWO LIVES

TUTANKHAMEN AND AFTER

THE LYNCHING BEE

POEMS 1914-1916

AESOP AND HYSSOP

THE VAUNT OF MAN AND OTHER POEMS

SONNETS AND POEMS

DRAMA

RED BIRD

GLORY OF THE MORNING

AUTOBIOGRAPHY

THE LOCOMOTIVE GOD

TRANSLATIONS

GILGAMESH: EPIC OF OLD BABYLONIA

BEOWULF

LUCRETIUS

BELGIUM AND GERMANY (from the Dutch of Dr. J. H. Labberton)

THE VALE OF CONTENT (from the German of Hermann Sudermann)

THE FRAGMENTS OF EMPEDOCLES

MISCELLANEOUS

LUCRETIUS (Latin text with introduction and commentary, in collaboration with Stanley B. Smith)

THE SCANSION OF MIDDLE ENGLISH ALLITERATIVE VERSE

BEOWULF AND THE NIBELUNGEN COUPLET

EL METRO DEL CID (in Spanish)

SOCRATES, MASTER OF LIFE

THE OREGON TRAIL OF FRANCIS PARKMAN (editor)

THE POET OF GALILEE

BYRON AND BYRONISM IN AMERICA

(1)